THE AFFLICTED GIRLS

THE AFFLICTED GIRLS

POEMS

Nicole Cooley

LOUISIANA STATE UNIVERSITY PRESS

BATON ROUGE

2004

Designer: Amanda McDonald Scallan
Typeface: Adone Caslon
Printer and binder: Thomsom-Shore, Inc.

Library of Congress Cataloging-in-Publication Data:

Cooley, Nicole.
    The afflicted girls : poems / Nicole Cooley.
       p. cm.
    ISBN 0-8071-2945-3 (alk. paper) — ISBN 0-8071-2946-1 (pbk. : alk. paper)
    1. Salem (Mass.)—History—Colonial period, ca. 1600–1775—Poetry. 2. Trials (Witchcraft)—Poetry. 3. Witch-
craft—Poetry. I. Title.
    PS3553.05647A37 2004
    811'.54—dc22   2003017043

The paper in this book meets the guidelines for permanence and durability of the Committee on Production Guide-
lines for Book Longevity of the Council on Library Resources. ∞

For my sister Alissa—with love beyond words to tell.

Witchcraft was hung, in History,
But History and I
Find all the Witchcraft that we need
Around us, every Day—

—EMILY DICKINSON, #1583

CONTENTS

ACKNOWLEDGMENTS

Grateful acknowledgment is made to the editors of the following magazines in which some of these poems first appeared, sometimes under different titles or in slightly different forms: *Black Warrior Review:* "Archival: Silence," "Archival: The Devil's Book"; *Common-Place: An Interactive Journal of Early American Life:* "The Mather Boys," "Witness, Recantation," "He or His Apparition"; *Luna: A Magazine of Poetry and Translation:* "Outbreak"; *Meridian:* "Prophecy" (under the title "Testimony: Prophecy"), "Testimony: Bride of Christ," "Genealogy"; *Missouri Review:* "John Winthrop: Reasons to be Considered for . . . the Intended Plantation in New England," "An Alphabet of Lessons for Girls," "Testimony: The Parris House," "Testimony: Spectral Evidence" (under the title "Witch Research: The Essex County Museum"), "Testimony: Escape," "Witness Tree"; *New England Review:* "Mary Warren's Sampler"; *Pleiades:* "The People vs. Bridget Bishop, 1999"; *Poetry Northwest:* "The Archive of the Future"; *Pool:* "The Great Migration, 1630"; *Proceedings of the American Antiquarian Society:* "Testimony: Talk Through Her Body," "The Salem Witch Trials Memorial," "Archival: Error, Imprint, Tear"; *Thirteenth Moon: A Feminist Literary Magazine:* "Sabbath Fragment"; *Virginia Quarterly Review:* "Testimony: The Invisible World," "Archival: In the Reading Room"; *Web Del Sol:* "The Wake of History," "The Waste Book"; *Women's Studies: An Interdisciplinary Journal:* "The Afflicted Girls," "The Afflicted Girls, New Orleans, 1978."

New Young American Poets Anthology, ed. Kevin Prufer (Carbondale: Southern Illinois University Press, 2000): "Mary Warren's Sampler," "Publick Fast on Account of the Afflicted: March 31, 1692," "Testimony: The Mother" (under the title "The Mother: Dorcas Good") and "John Winthrop: Reasons to be Considered for . . . the Intended Plantation in New England."

It is a pleasure to thank the many people who helped me with this book. Many thanks to the editorial staff at LSU Press, especially Virginia Willis. For a creative artist's fellowship and the gift of sustaining faith in this project, I will always be thankful to the American Antiquarian Society. Joanne Chaison, John Hench, Jim Moran, and Caroline Sloat at AAS were instrumental in supporting this book. I would also like to thank Elizabeth Reis and Bernard Rosenthal for their reading of these poems and for their help with historical background. This work was supported in part by grants from Bucknell University, the City University of New York's PSC-CUNY Research Award Program, and the Presidential Research Award at Queens College-CUNY. In addition to thanking my colleagues at Bucknell University and Queens College, I am especially grateful to Beverly Achille, Pamela Barnett, Nancy Comley, Maureen Cummins, Amelie Hastie, Carrie Hintz, Cynthia Hogue, Victoria Pitts, Talia Schaffer, Suzanne Schneidau, Harold Schweizer, Renée Sentilles, Stacey Waite, and John Weir for their encouragement of this project. Deepest gratitude to Jacki Cooley, Josh Cooley, Peter Cooley, and Mary Leader, and, especially, to Julia Kasdorf and Gretchen Mattox. Alex Hinton was this book's first reader. Without his love and generosity, this book would never have been written. And Meridian—as if these poems could have willed her here.

PREFACE

In late 1691 in the middle of a cold, bleak New England winter, several young girls from Salem Village refused to eat, they choked, they lost their powers of speech, sight and hearing, they claimed they were bitten and pinched by unseen bodies. Based on their array of symptoms, a doctor made the diagnosis: the evil hand is upon them. Hereafter, they would be known as the afflicted girls. Who torments you? the Reverend Samuel Parris asked, and the girls began to answer.

In the summer of 1692, nineteen people and two dogs were executed by hanging, one man was pressed to death, and more than 150 people were sent to prison, where several, including a baby born in jail, died.

Cotton Mather wrote: No place that I know of has got such a spell upon it, as will always keep the devil out.

Archival: Silence

A slipcase keeps the book of voices safe
till I untie the string holding the broken

spine together   Then I wait
When the pages open on the table
they could crack into pieces

On Gallows Hill rope burns the neck
before the body breaks   Up
on the scaffolding   Have you last words?

I don't have words   because I'm nothing
but a collection of evidence   stories splintered in all

directions   voices I can't fasten
to the page   history

disappearing before I write it down
Say it   Unsay it

History choked me   History took hold
of my throat

John Winthrop, "Reasons to be Considered for . . . the Intended Plantation in New England," 1629

Who is the Author of Disaster?
   For an answer, read
      The Book of Nature or
         a woman's face.

the whole earth is the Lord's garden

Who will guide us
   out of Egypt, over the Red Sea
      the color of shame
         into the New Jerusalem?

this land grows weary of her inhabitants

England was the lover
   you must leave behind,
      the New World is your wife,
         her body the City on the Hill.

the church hath no place left to fly but into the wilderness

Split the trees at the root,
   slash the salt grass to clear
      a long road to the future.
         Lock your wife in the house.

Keep yourself safe.
Remember that the Invisible World is full of women.

An Alphabet of Lessons for Girls

As long as there is a contrary seed, a seed of the Woman,
and a seed of the Serpent, there will be opposition,
more or less, open or secret.
—REVEREND SAMUEL PARRIS, Sermon in Salem Village, January 3, 1692

A young girl should always be prepared to die.
Beware of a black man who would make you a handmaiden of the Devil.
Come to God willingly and quietly as if he were your husband.
Disagree with no man for men know the best and truest path.
Egg-in-a-glass will show your future husband's calling, but this trick is witchcraft.
Fast to find the road of correction on the Sabbath.
Graveyards are a place to remember that the Lord takes all girls' souls.
Houses where no women be are like deserts or untilled land.
Indians are evil men who will harm you, just as New England was once the Devil's
    land.
Judge not a man's deeds or thoughts, only let him judge you.
Keep silence when in the meeting house with men.
Look to your father, brother or master for guidance.
Milk will curdle and butter will turn to wool if you are a witch.
New Jerusalem is our paradise and no place for daughters of the Devil.
Obedience is a good wife's finest virtue.
Pins mark the hems of dresses and must never be used to prick the skin of men.
Question the Lord's good work and be cast out of Salem Village.
Reckless speech will lead you into temptation.
Satan is the prince of Lies, and witches are his servants.
Tying a woman neck and heels will cure her of the sin of witchcraft.
Unknown to witches is the power and light of God.
Vengeance against witchcraft is justice.
Witches' daughters must be witches themselves.
eXhort the Lord to save you by your confession of witchcraft.
Your name is blotted out of God's Book because you are a witch.
Zion will not be our true paradise till we have purged the witches from our land.

The Great Migration, 1630

Picture shipwreck and we never
arrive. Imagine the edge
of the bay, bubbles like a crown

of hair. Invent a bad angel
who guides the ship off
course, down to the ocean floor.

Conjure crosswinds and a dark
blank sky, and the hull's wood
splinters like a fistful

of matches. Sails collapse,
while Angel steps closer,
loosens the folds of his coat.

Watch Angel empty
the landscape: pitched ropes tip
the deck, hammocks unravel.

No shore in sight.

See Angel open his arms, his skin
milk, chest flattened into
a map of the New World.

Let the ship's sinking save us.

But the ship sails on, intact,
and far from the harbor,
in the graveyard
salt grass thickens the stone wall.

Prophecy

ANN PUTNAM, JR.

Hold the dandelion, pale halo, all stalk. Listen
to the lesson: blow the white seeds into the wind to see if your mother wants you.
        My mother lies in bed all day.

                In the brushwood booth,
        far from her, I invent my own church for the other
children, make them kneel in the dirt while I recite from
Revelations:

Fear none of those things which thou shalt suffer:
        behold, the devil shall cast some of you into prison.

Childbed fever claimed my aunt, cousins born
    dead. Now I offer my warnings to the girls. I speak my sermon.

Our family leads this village. In the meetinghouse without my mother, we sit
    up front. *And he shall rule them with a rod of iron; as the vessels of a potter shall*

              they be broken to slivers. Before me,
    the girls wait for me to lead the prayers. I tell them heaven
will crack open like a broken mixing bowl and they'll be judged.

Remember therefore how Thou hast received and heard
    and hold fast and repent. I explain: labor is the punishment

for Eve's first sin. But if a baby is born dead,
    someone afflicts you. The girls in the front row nod.

He that overcometh, the same shall be clothed in white
    raiment; and I will not blot out his name of the book of life, but I will confess
              his name before my Father. I describe

the Devil's Book, the man in black who says
        he's from the Golden City, who will hurt
            the village children. I lay the dandelions in the grass,

          seeds blown out, like green-tipped matches.
      And he said unto me, thou must prophesy again
    before my peoples, and nations, and tongues and kings.

And I ask the girls: do you love your mothers? do you want your mothers' babies
    dying?
Do you want to cure
                        this world of these infections?

Directions for Ordering the Voice

Walk along the river's margin, all salt grass
to the neck

of land between Collins Cove and dull gray water.
Cross into town

toward Essex, past isinglass and brickwork, weather-
boards, a window's

leaded edges where light breaks into diamonds
and a girl's trundle

fits under her mother's mattress like a drawer. Rain
stutters on the grass.

Remember the bed imprinted with body after body.
Remember the shelf

crowded with local histories, maps to the past. Pretend
to remember

how once fear seeped into a house like rusty water,
how a mother's

sickbed was strung with cords, cat's cradle. How once
a girl–

How the voices will pass through. Remember you are no one
in this story.

Outbreak

As if land could be a body

As if its skin could swell and stretch and blister

As if under a scab of grass blood stops in its tracks

As if the road's loose stones catch   gag in the river's throat

As if the field is a mother   nipples leaking milk   hard with infection

As if the village is an eye   shut tight   iris flecked with mucous   but still watching

As if the Devil is an Indian   as if the Devil never found his way to Salem Village
before this year

As if I could hold the book   open the box   unfold the map's blurred edges   bring
back this whole lost story

The Afflicted Girls

know what they want: just this fury
of happiness. It's the refrain of men's voices

saying their names, it's their testimony
on their own mother's tongues,

it's their words repeating like a hand slapping
a girl's face, over and over.

Abigail. Mary. Mercy, Elizabeth.
Who said vengeance? They love

the meetinghouse's cold, whitewashed walls
where their accusations scrawl and climb

the surface in beautiful script. *She's a witch,*
a witch. I name her as a witch.

No girls in Salem Village are allowed to go to school.
No girls can hold

a writing tablet on their laps, eggshell white,
color of the nightgowns

they are taught to sew. No girls hope for a place
in memory.

Who said vengeance? We know what they want:

to speak in unison

to have a single voice

to inhabit this one body all the way to the future.

Archival: Fantasy

Here is a book, the pages tied together with wire, here
is a testimony, how a man gripped his wife's wrist
to search for teeth marks, straight pins, in her skin,

here is the museum where I imagine the box of evidence,
wedding sampler unraveling to a girl's shaking stitches,
hymnal, sleeve of a muslin dress, where I want to hold this history

in my hands, say, here is the world without us, call to the past,
come back, teach me, till the voices knock together like bodies
turning over and over in another room, and here is marriage

where the sheets smell like cold dirt, where I want to pull you
down below the floor, below the ground, where
a death warrant's red seals the future like a print of a wax kiss.

Testimony: The Parris House

BETTY PARRIS

I press my mouth between
the boards, the floor's single
planks above the parlor ceiling,
watch Father pray
for the safety of the village below.

Our Lord Jesus Christ knows how many Devils there are in his church and who they are.

Fire blooms in the brick chimney
in the room where Mama sleeps
all day, where I am not allowed.
In the doorway I play dolls,
line up the little girls
for church, force their bodies
face down, make them pray.

Come this day to the Lord's table, lest Satan enter more powerfully into you—lest while the bread be between your teeth the wrath of the Lord come pouring down upon you.

The middle of winter—I am not allowed
to leave the house.
In secret, I've touched my tongue
to a clot of ice,
swallowed snow from the frozen field
behind the parsonage.

The church consists of good and bad: as a garden that has weeds as well as flowers.

Not allowed to leave
the house, I know
how to twist an egg's split shell
to reveal the future in a glass:
a husband, a man in Black
who opens his arms
and carries me to the Golden City.

Pray we also that not one true saint may suffer as a devil either in name or body.

In the Golden City, in summer,
all the girls are dolls. Cornstalk

child. Apple doll. Cloth poppet stuck
with pins. I am the wooden girl
running through the fields all night.

We are either saints or devils: The Scripture gives us no medium.

Strings of egg white swirl
into the shape of a man's face.
Mama will sleep all day. Father
will kneel forever on the parlor floor.
The wooden girl will run away.

Yea, and in our land—in this and some neighboring places—how many, what multi-
tudes of witches and wizards, has the devil instigated with utmost violence to attempt
the overthrow of religion?

I press my mouth to the floor.

One of you is a Devil.

Testimony: The Wake of History

TITUBA

The sky is a palm spread open, sheltering
nobody. An egg-yolk yellow moon floats over
the cage of men
in the middle of Bridgetown's market: a display
of runaway slaves. When I walk along the margin

of the beach, I don't look at them.
I don't look at *Gift of God,* the waiting ship,
its principal cargo salted fish, sugar, slaves.
Instead I watch the water stutter against rocks.

⌒

In Salem, the New World sticks to my tongue
like wool. I can't breathe
in the Reverend's house. I can't sleep
in the bed beside his daughter,
her flushed skin limned with sweat
in the cold room.

Each morning, Family Prayer, a circle
of bowed heads as the Reverend explains
the fallen world, this land infected by black devils.

Afterward I walk to the marsh to watch
the water separating here from home.
The sky shuts its fist.

⌒

In the dark, feel along the edge
of history's body
to find the place in which local legend
becomes the truest story.

Touch the small, painful ache
where myths originate.
Rub your fingers on it like a scab.

The Examination of Titibe

(H) Titibe what evil spirit have you familiarity with
(T) none
(H) why do you hurt these children
(T) I do not hurt them
(H) who is it then
(T) the devil for ought I know

The Reverend's hand spreads open over my back.
He could reach inside
my body, drag words from my lungs,
force my silence out.

His fingers circle my wrists. His ribs
lock over mine, press me against the pantry wall.
His voice, pure threat. *Confess.*

Upstairs, his daughter spins and twists
in bed, calls out my name.
Later I will hold her tightly
while she shudders in my lap.

(H) doe you see who it is that torments these children now
(T) yes it is goode good she hurts them in her own shape
(H) & who is it that hurts them now
(T) I am blind noe I cannot see

Find the gap,
the rip in the paper. Pull out the stitches.
Stretch open the loops of thread.

Wait in the pantry, the garden
where she once waited.
Follow the path's wet slate to the harbor.

Stand on the rocks and let go of the story.
The body sinks to the soft ocean floor.

❧

Here is the fallen world. Here is the village
where children choke and cry out
in their sleep, as her voice breaks
in the shore's throat, as fiction spins into fact.

Testimony: Bride of Christ

ELIZABETH ELDRIDGE PARRIS

Like an altar the world beyond my window
is spread with winter's good white cloth.
My husband's prayers leak through the ceiling,
into my bed, inside my body.
He calls us One Flesh. My lungs are burning.
I can't breathe in this house. I can't
hold my daughter close enough, her skin
sticky with a film of fever beside me
in the marriage bed. *The Head of the Woman
is the Man. The Wife is the Weaker Vessel.*
In my arms, Betty reaches for me in sleep,
and I remember the world before this one,
Bridgetown's air heavy with water, me
on my knees on the edge of the white beach.
My lungs are burning. He says I must
reverence him. Once, Obedience was
a small stone of pain he forced inside
my body. Once, Duty stuck like a bone
in my throat. Once, rocks split the ocean
into two separate directions. We are
One Flesh. I can't get out of bed.
My husband says Sin infects this village,
but his words infect my daughter.
To save her, I remember my secret prayer, how
the sand burned my skin. Secret: I don't believe
in him or God, Head of the Family, Master
of the Parsonage, Father of us all.
But all last winter, in bed, I worked
the sampler he named *Tree of Life:* stiff
oak latched with apples and the names
of womanly virtues: *Love, Honor, Truth,
Silence.* He says wives should submit
to their husbands like men to God.
My daughter shudders in my arms.
She is afflicted and what I pray for now
is natural sleep while his sermons split
the roof beams of this house. The word
of God requires: a husband rules. We

must give up, let his prayers fill our mouths.
Marriage is the punishment he invented
for the wicked in this village: split stick pressing
the tongue flat, forcing the voice back
inside the body. My lungs are burning.
Bury my words in the dirt.

Publick Fast on Account of the Afflicted: March 31, 1692

If we eat, we choke. Bread wedges in our throats.
Peas are pins

that prick the tongue. Mothers' milk burns our lungs
as if we're drowning.

We gag and gag until the Reverend vows to cure this village:
together, every family

will fast and pray to drive the witches out of here.
In the meeting house,

the Sacrament cracks on the black plate. The Reverend reads.
Dear Lord, Receive

Our Souls. Take Our Mortal Bodies. Save These Afflicted.
We wait, shoulder

to shoulder, lean together in the pew like sisters. *Abigail.*
Mary. Mercy. Elizabeth.

Our secret circles us, keeping us safe. The whitewashed walls
block out the sun,

yet we four see beyond the visible—We dream
the witches' Black Mass Meal:

milk sweetened with spit. Finger bones folded under the skin
of a pudding.

Urine-drizzled gruel. We agree: the witches tear bread as if
it were girls' flesh.

Abigail. Mary. Mercy. Elizabeth. As if the bread were our bodies.
We'll tell the story.

We'll choke, hold our throats closed with our breath, until
the women disappear.

The Reverend doesn't know but our love fills us, links us
like a line of paper dolls.

The candles burn and burn and burn. Against the other women,
we are one body.

Testimony: The Mother

DORCAS GOOD

Snow fills the fields like milk.
Inside the Meeting House I wait on the communion table.
I unbutton my muslin dress while the Reverend reads

To the Marshall of Essex or his Deputy:
You are in their Magistrates' names hereby required
to bring before us Dorcas Good.

I am four years old. My dress drops from my body.
The three girls circle, calling
the mother, the mother, holding their throats with their hands.

I close my eyes: I'm outside in the snow,
standing in the harbor's dark throat we followed
here, to the New Jerusalem.

Or I'm with my mother in Ipswich Jail.

The Reverend holds a candle close
to each girl's wrist, to the teeth marks in a row,
like tiny stitches, they say are mine.

                    In jail, my mother pulls
me into her lap, cradles my head against her chest
as my mouth reaches for her nipple.

Here is the Devil's Mark, the Reverend raises
my hand for all to see. A small red bite.
A perfect circle on my palm.

Did a yellow bird suck here between your fingers?

                    I close my eyes
and the bird spreads its wings
on my mother's shoulders, hiding us, keeping us safe.

Now, Child, repeat the prayer.
On the table, my arms stretched out:
Our Father, Which Art in Heaven, Hallowed Be Thy Name.

I could be a bird. The girls still circle.
When I look at them they fall against each other
like the rag dolls my mother arranged on my bed at home.

                           I want to be invisible.
I want to go back to my mother's body.

Branches snap off the black trees on Gallows Hill.
Ice cracks on the roof of the jail.
This girl is a witch. The men in the front pew nod.

The girls let go of their throats.
Does my mother sleep in jail alone?   I want to call to her.
I can't. My body stands straight and still on the examining table,

                               my voice torn out—

Testimony: Spectral Evidence

SAMUEL GRAY

I wake to light and a woman
who stands beside my bed.

She is not my wife.

Outside—winter I lock
my door against, wood planked tight
to keep the wind out.

She Afflicts me. She is not my wife.

Her kiss belongs to him,
her breath cold blistering my mouth.

In the name of God what do you come for?

The baby sees her, screams in the cradle.
Within three months, my child will die.

She is not my wife.

It is the Devil. The body belongs
to Bridget Bishop.

The Mather Boys

RICHARD, INCREASE, COTTON

The one who starts it: who first crosses the cold lead ocean to settle in this land

The one who prays and fasts in secret for God to untie his tongue

The one who waits all day in his study for proof of Election or at least a Remedy

The one whose ship is driven against the white rocks at the edge of Isle of Shoals

The one with an Infirmity in his Speech, each word splitting open in his mouth

The one who leaves his study only for meals or Family Prayer

The one whose hand crosses the page again and again, practicing words he
cannot say

The one who holds *The Book of Martyrs* on the ship's slick deck as anchor cables
snap, sails rip from masts

The one who explains that *Strong affections bring strong afflictions* and shuts his
study door, his son standing alone outside

The son who dreams his grandfather's voyage, who reads his father's prayers, who
will write the future down:

It is a world all over defiled with Sin, God will shortly burn it for a Witch

Witness, Recantation

For Elizabeth Reis

> I enjoy, though in abundance of afflictions,
> being close confined here in a loathsome dungeon.
> —MARGARET JACOBS, letter to her father from
>   Salem prison, August 21, 1692

Honored Father, when I remember you

your eyes turn the color of a bruise.
As soon as you speak to me you disappear,
and I have to imagine
the ocean that might lie between us,

then something breaks inside my body
and everyone I've hurt returns:
Grandfather, Mother, You,
skin translucent like the oiled paper
we stretched in place of glass
between the window lead.

I see through your body. You never
have to say it: *Lying is a sin.*
What's worse to you, false testimony
or a wrong confession? Down here is all
darkness, the only sound the slur
of rain in the dirt, water rats scratching
inside the walls. Grandfather is dead.

Mother locked in Boston Jail. You
escaped. *Lying is a sin.* Just as any telling
of this story is a lie,

                    just as in the future,
years from now when you and I are dead,
another woman will write this letter down
in a room with sky-colored walls
and electric candles under a water-
color of the sea, waves capped in white
like dress lace, a girl on the dock waving

goodbye to no one under the caption:
Salem, Massachusetts, New England's Maritime Paradise.

He or His Apparition

About noon, at Salem, Giles Corey was press'd to death
for standing Mute.
—SAMUEL SEWALL, *Diary*, September 19, 1692

The girls' testimony is gravel scattered on the grass.

Ann Putnam: *Giles Corey or his Apperance has most greviously afflected me by beating
pinching and almost Choaking me to death*

Inside the meetinghouse each afflicted girl repeats the next.

Mercy Lewis: *I veryly beleve in my heart that Giles Cory is a dreadfull wizzard for
sence he had ben in prison he or his Apperance has come and most greviously tormented me*

The copier flattens the page, hammers down identical speech.

Sarah Bibber: *I have ben most greviously affleted by giles Cory or his Appearance*

But the man won't speak to defend or plead. He sits still and silent in his pew.

Mary Warren: *At the time of his examination I saw: s'd Cory or his appeirition
most: dredfully afflect: Mary Walcot An putnam. Mercy lewes & Sarah Vibber*

The morning of his execution: the meetinghouse floods with light.
Outside a circle rises around the punished man:
the magistrates pile stone after stone on his ribs to crush him into speech.

Nobody can see the lesson: nothing can drive the voice out of the body.

Testimony: Escape, July 30, 1692

NATHANIEL CARY

1. Forecast

The minister begins with prayer.
The Afflicted sit
together—two of the girls
cannot be more than ten.
Beside me, Elizabeth is still,
her fingers twisted into mine,
into a single fist.
We are here to see
if the Afflicted know her.
The minister begins with prayer.

2. Dream

You woke in the night to describe
the other country
where you'd gone without me:
not England, not the New Jerusalem,
but a world of women
in the wilderness, a family
of mothers, daughters, wives
who belonged to no one.
Then you turned away from me.

3. At the Ordinary

On either side of the pine table we wait.
When the girls enter the alehouse
they tumble on the floor
like swine, they cry out
Cary.
The name's sound fills the room,
floats through the roof,
settles on the fields like ash.

4. The Lord's Prayer

Forced to stand, her arms stretched out,
she is not allowed to lean

against me. I am forbidden
to hold her hands.

She had strength enough
to torment those persons,
and she should have strength enough
to stand.

Our Father, Which Art in Heaven,
Hallowed be Thy Name.
Her voice shakes like a tree in the wind.
I cannot touch her.

5. Dream

Outside the meeting house I watch the men
huddle together in late-afternoon sun
as they tell their story—

I woke up and the woman
had pressed herself against my chest.
She held me down. She sucked
my breath out of my throat.

I couldn't scream. I couldn't move.
She was not my wife. She was a witch.

6. Cambridge Jail

As if the body weighed down is safe.
As if she could rise from the dirt floor
to afflict the sleeping town.
As if leg irons eight pounds each
could stop panic, cure the girls.

I am allowed to visit once.
I cannot touch her.

7. *Complaint*

but to speak of their usage of the Prisoners, and their Inhumanity shewn to them, at the time of their Execution, no sober Christian could bear; they had also tryals of cruel mockings; which is the more considering what a People for Religion, I mean the profession of it, we have been

I acquainted her with her danger.

8. *The Lord's Prayer*

I am not allowed to hold her hands.

9. *Dream*

I close my eyes and she unfolds her body over mine.

10. *Providence*

Beyond my life without you will be our escape.

Past the thin frame walls of the jail, past
the meetinghouse, the tavern, another world—

Rhode Island wilderness, a house to hold us
made of latched pine branches, bed of leaves

where we will lie down alone together,
bed where we'll tell story after story

to make you safe.

Sabbath Fragment

THE COMMUNION TABLE

Each examination, I hold them down. I press their bodies
                to my surface—smooth wood etched with scratches
   where the girls marked signatures
       in secret: *X* equaling
              Abigail and Mary and Mercy and Elizabeth.

Each Day of Rest in the middle of Winter:
          Bible spread open, white wings pressed flat against me,
   men and women waiting on the benches, bricks
                   wrapped in wool between their feet.
                                 And the Reverend's voice:
We'll rid this village of the Devil. We'll crush the lies out of their bodies.
                                     The four girls nod.

A brick breaks bones. Rope snaps a neck. I hold them down.

The bodies: I wear their silence.

The girls: I am their language.

Testimony: The Invisible World
COTTON MATHER

> I have indeed set myself to countermine the whole plot of the Devil
> against New England, in every Branch of it, as far as one of my
> Darkness can comprehend such a Work of Darkness.
> —COTTON MATHER, *Wonders of the Invisible World*

Each word weighted my mouth, my voice
lodged in my throat like a stone.
A stammerer, my father said, *may the Lord untie his tongue.*

Each syllable dragged out on a rope,
sentence by slow sentence, a diary entry:
today another SECRET fast and alone

in my room I begged to reach God, prayed not
to be SPEECHLESS. For a week in bed
I waited for a sign. Each night

I swore to use my tongue as the Lord's
and not my own. And so he brought the trials.
Each word became a body hung at the neck,

branch snapped off a tree. *Five witches*
were lately executed impudently demanding
of God a Miraculous Vindication of their Innocency.

Now the Devil has joined the Visible World.
Now God's Book is shut, his Covenant broken.

Now my voice is a fist that splits the sky.

Mary Warren's Sampler

You were a little while ago an Afflicted person,
now you are an Afflicter: How comes this to pass?
—JUDGE HATHORNE and JUDGE CORWIN

Reversible Stitches: my mother and I leaned over a single piece of English linen
— I want her smooth white hands not my master's fingers pinching the skin along
my backbone voice breathing *Mary* — Single Satin Stitch — I stand before the
court and I say *I am sorry for it I am sorry* and the girls shut their eyes — at home he
struck my arm I hid behind the spinning wheel I hid from him — Chain Stitch —
I gripped my mother's wrist her cold hand folded on the sheet of the bed we shared
— *I will tell I will tell* — he said he'd thrash the Devil out of me he said he'd drown
me in the creek behind the barn — Lace Filling Stitch — Mother's pattern book
open on my lap I copied *A Noble and Generous Fear Proceeds From Love* in silk
thread — I licked my finger my black spit leaked onto the page — the girls at any
moment will fall down together hands set at their throats to show I am a witch —
My master's iron tongs could burn me out of my fit — Fishbone Stitch — my
mother bent over the cloth head bowed to tie each small knot I touched her gleam-
ing hair — In the court I bite my lips and whisper the lesson *Fear Proceeds From
Love Love is Fear* — Buttonhole Stitch — he told me *If you are Afflicted I wish you
were more Afflicted* — My fingers blackened bread and butter when I set his table
and I screamed — Backstitch To the Past — to the edge of Eve's body we arranged
at the sampler's border — to Fear to the marks along my arm his fingers made like
stitches — he called me his *Jade* his body crushing mine until — Darning Stitch
Cross Stitch Loop Stitch — *I will tell I will tell It was the Devil's book my master
Proctor brought to me* — as witness my hand Mary Warren

Archival: The Devil's Book

Vellum is skin   you want
to believe   you say the book

you touch could be a body

you say you could travel
back to that past

where a girl's hand blurs
the surface of the Devil's Book

I touched it with my fingers

where the girl's signature is only
an X like her mother's body

where daughter accuses mother
and then the girl confesses

the book was red
the paper of it was white

Archival: Video Diary

For Amelie Hastie

First Direction   aim and shoot the girls   stand back

(God's Kingdom is a mock-up of the afflicted tacked
to the wall of the editing room)

Close-up on the cast   shot composed like a family portrait

What you're making here is not the museum
display   voice-over directing now turn now turn

Give each girl her lines

(In God's Kingdom the story is wound tight on tape
its invisible strip spiraling to another century)

Aim and shoot the girls standing together in a row

Frame after frame will set the past in motion
but the script requires a moment of direct address

(the poem wants to stage the drama
contained in the screen's clean rectangle of light)

So on the last day invent your own museum

Then add the voices and the tape loops backward
to hold the girls' lost speech

Then cut to the moment when I fling
my voice out into the fields   down history's corridor
crowded with everything that has already been said

The Waste Book
For Bernard Rosenthal

must always be recopied twice,
the pen a shovel turning the earth's surface, opening

the page to another version of history.
In the meetinghouse a man corrects

church records, head bent to the paper
that will offer us this past, this

story, while at the end of another century,
a woman watches her study window

like a movie screen, her garden's beds
turning to torn, yellowed paper. She is ready

to erase her own story, cross out
her voice, blur her words to nothing

but stiff ink. What relief, she thinks,
to step outside her body, to leave

herself, to transcribe the archive's directions:

one or two words missing.
name illegible, possibly John.
name completely missing.
this whole last line has been struck out.

as if only the voices hold her own speech
together, as if the voices cancel out her own.

In the other century, pages stack and settle
as the man works alone all night, retracing

parish records like a repeated prayer:

August 28 by an Order from the Governor
and Council was observed as a day of Fasting
and Prayer, to seek mercy from God in relation
to the present afflicted state of things in both Englands.

We should know the woman
is all wrong when she calls the past an empty

plate she can rinse clean, snow-covered
road she watches from her window.

No—each page marks a plot, a burial ground,
each word a seed needling the dirt.

The Afflicted Girls, New Orleans, 1978

For Elizabeth Zervigon

Bruise on the girl's backbone, contusion
their fingers pressure under, into
her ribs, her spine. They believe a spirit
will lift her from this carpet the color

of baby aspirin, from this house,
this middle-school sleepover.
Light as a feather, stiff as a board.
See how the girl rises, see how the others can

fake any magic: Dexedrine licked
off a tracing paper, off a half-
drawn map of New England, where none
of them have been. Heat drums against

their necks. They want to believe a spirit
can lift them out of themselves. They want
to believe they lift each other. Light
as a feather. Last year, they practiced tongue

kissing on each other's hands. Last year,
they were children. Now they're grown up:
they know how to hurt each other.
I call back to the girls.   I say, don't stay

here, forever, on this small square of floor,
believing only in your own fists, your fingers.
Stand up. Walk out. Let your voices lunge and stagger
all the long way out of childhood.

The People vs. Bridget Bishop, July 1999

In Salem, the history of America comes alive.
—Mayor Stanley J. Usovicz, Jr.

Judge Hathorne wears black nylon socks, and the kid playing Goodman Lauder
has slicked his hippie ponytail flat. Beside them on stage, Bridget looks bored by
her arrest. "You, the assembly, will decide her innocence or guilt," the Reverend
Parris says. In our folding chairs, we wait.

We are tourists. We are the citizens of Salem Village.

"How do we defeat the devil?" Judge Hathorne asks the crowd. Bridget's hands
are chained, the key to release her held by a twelve-year-old in the front row. In
the back, I'm taking notes. I write everything down. "I'm innocent as a child un-
born," Bridget tells the court.

We are the audience. We are here for testimony.

Goodwife Sheldon tightens a macramé shawl around her shoulders. Bridget
slumps, stares straight out at us, red bodice laced tight over her breasts. I'm trying
to step out of this summer's heat, return to a winter at the end of another century.
Crossing the page again and again, my hand blurs ink. "She oppressed him,"
Judge Hathorne explains, signaling a man beside him. Reverend Parris has
changed costumes: now he's a farmer in a three-cornered felt hat.

We are the witnesses. We are her jury.

Goodman and Goodwife Cook walk together to the center of the stage. Bridget's
off the shoulder blouse belongs to a flamenco dancer, and her long, loose hair is
wrong. "I am innocent to a witch. I know not what a witch is."

We take pictures. We videotape. We write everything down.

A child beside me wants to know, "Could any of these events have been a
dream?" This is my question too. "Good People, what say you?" Judge Hathorne
paces under a red sign glowing EXIT. "What say you about this woman?"

We are the citizens of Salem Village. No—we're not—

And before we stumble outside to sunlight, back to our cars, we will vote her
guilty: 38 to 12. *How do we defeat the devil?* We don't. But we will name him in
the body of a woman again and again.

Witness Tree

Salem's first false Spring: the tree
spikes the sky, a split tongue,
an emblem of Grief. Who has lost
a child? The village women whisper,

I saw her stand between the cradle and the bed.
I saw her red dress flash, a candle
flicker when I spoke her name.
Bridget. You, Bridget Bishop, killed my child.

I wait beside the tree; I will her to come back
yet I see nothing beyond the tree, trunk
honed to a point like an old tooth.
Who has never lost a child? Who has never

seen a graveyard bordered with the smallest stones?
Who has never chronicled the body's
breaking open to reveal its secret?
Here, ice creaks, a whisper, *Lies, Lies,*

and the ailanthus blooms too soon,
red petals insuring its death. I stood
between the cradle and the bed: the child
was missing. The child was never there.

I covered my breasts with a square
of red, in mourning, pictured the trench
of earth where the men lowered each small coffin.
Snuff out the candle, say her name,

pretend my body is unfamiliar, swelling
beneath my hands, my dress. Of course it's wrong:
I didn't see but I imagine.
I want to ask her about the children

or who drove the tree into the earth or
which God could choose these afflictions?
Ice breaks, leaves snake from branches,
bright jade. Water pools in the grass.

She killed my child, the women say. I lean
against the trunk and the tree speaks back:

I remember her as the first body when
body after body was cut down
from me, laid flat in the dirt. No grave was dug.
No prayers were ever whispered.

I have no child. Everyone in this story is dead.
I am a knife cracking open this too blue sky.

Testimony: Talk Through Her Body

DORCAS GOOD

Ice etches the river like a stick on a broken slate.
My mother's body does not belong
to me. In jail, a yellow bird

                    sleeps in her arms,
sucks her milk as I once did. Her nipple is a finger
where the Devil holds on.

The Reverend says the way to the soul
is a woman's body: if you are willing Satan just slips in.
Now at home alone

I sketch the moment she became a witch.

The Reverend says the Devil claimed my mother
because she opened herself to him.
I rub her out with my fist.

My mother is a clapboard house,
cold splitting planks. Or she's a field the Devil
cuts a clean road through.

My mother's body does not belong to me.

The afflicted girls own it. They crowd
around her. They are a wall, a fence circling
a small, empty plot of dirt.

Now I erase the slate. My mother is

a candle on the table
                    beside me, flame guttering out.

Genealogy

Are you a descendent? the woman at the poetry reading asks.
She unfolds

her own family tree, blue ink linking her to Salem's past
like veins under

the palest skin. *The Nurse family or Susannah Martin's line?*
I shake my head,

but I don't tell her how I wish family were something to try
on, a borrowed

wedding dress. I can't explain how the branches of my family tree
split at the root

into silence, into blank spaces on the page. I won't describe
Reverse World,

the game my sister and I played on the ceiling of our room,
how we lay side

by side together to name an orphanage of little girls,
their tiny beds lined

up and linked like letters of the alphabet. The ceiling was
our writing

paper, family a lesson in penmanship, a story written
in someone else's

beautiful sloping script. Now my sister is the one with me
in the archive

when I look up alone to watch my own hand crossing,
recrossing these pages,

when I tell myself the past is a new world I can write
for us to live in.

The Archive of the Future

For Alex Hinton

1. *Egg in a Glass*

predicts the future, all girls know.
Here is how we choose our husbands:

crack the egg against the edge
of the looking glass, spill the white over the mirror.
You'll see your future husband's face.

Or the shape of a coffin. Or the body
of a woman whose glance can kill a man,
curdle milk inside a cow,
turn churned butter into a sheet of wool.

2. *The Body of the Accused Bridget Bishop is Due to be Examined by the Magistrate of Salem Village at 6 O'clock in the Meeting House on the Communion Table.*

The goodwives of Salem Village whisper what their husbands told:

She pinched. She bit his skin
till a bruise blossomed,
purple petals spreading to the sky like fingers.

3. *Marriage*

In bed at the motel we stop spinning to remember.

The last night before I left
I climbed on top of you as if I could weigh you down
with my own body,
as if my hands were stones pressing you into the ground.

My breath stopped.
My throat choked.
I wanted to prove to you that I'd come back.

In the archive, in the bottom of a box
I find the goodwife and man
side by side in miniature,
painted into a frame
the size of a child's hand.

The past comes back.
The pages of the book open on the table.

Memory is a warning, a winding sheet
the woman in the doorway drops
to show her body to the man

as their future breaks across the glass.

Archival: In the Reading Room

Circle of Light:
inside my world turns safely miniature and a cart clatters over
gravel to drag the narrative out of that century

Pine Table:
book as big as a matchbox keeps the past contained and bordered
by a blue-edged mourning paper

Glass Room:
summer narrows to exclude anything but a snap as the book
clasps shut like a necklace

Desire:
to have no body
to become the book lying open on the cradle

To Stay Here
To watch these words subtract the world around them

The Salem Witch Trials Memorial

The memorial is a small plot of land.
Locust trees shade the benches built with broken stone.
The threshold reads: *My life lies in your hands.*

Bridget Bishop, Hanged June 10, 1692

Each bench conceals a body that's not there, an absence
I am wholly innocent of such wickedness.
once memorialized in a hole on Gallows Hill, the land

Sarah Good, Hanged July 19, 1692

you're told is now a playground. Look: understand
I can deny it to my dying day
you must read the threshold, touch each stone with your hands.

Rebecca Nurse, Hanged July 19, 1692

You're a trespasser into someone else's past and,
I am no witch
still, memory is nothing but this cold dirt, a plot of land.

George Burroughs, Hanged August 19, 1692

The voices are interrupted by the rock wall circling the sand.
Oh Lord Help me—
Listen: wait on the threshold. In your hands

John Proctor, Hanged August 19, 1692

you hold your notebook, your camera, to record history.
Later at home you can fast-forward to the past,
and you'll remember nothing but the story's plot, no land
where the threshold reads: the past is all lies written in your hand.

Archival: Error, Imprint, Tear

The book gives back more than the story

Words crossed-out   sentences crosshatched like stitches
endpapers ripped   name carefully erased
____ ____ Her Book   a girl's curving signature

I want to carry this world with me
but the story keeps dissolving in my hands   and the book

is no open road to let me travel back

                                        The book is a voice trying to speak

The book is a gash of light

NOTES

"John Winthrop, 'Reasons to be Considered for . . . the Intended Plantation in New England,' 1629"
In "Reasons to Be Considered For Justifying the Undertakers of the Intended Plantation in New England and For Encouraging Such Whose Hearts God Shall Move to Join With Them In It," first governor of the Massachusetts Bay Colony, John Winthrop, carefully explains his reasons for a Puritan settlement in the New World to counter challengers who think no one should travel to New England, this "wilderness," this "heathen place."

"Prophecy"
Italicized text taken from the book of Revelation.

"Directions for Ordering the Voice"
The title is a phrase from *The Bay Psalm Book* (1640), the Massachusetts Bay Colony's new translation of the psalms and the first book printed in "English America."

"Testimony: The Parris House"
Italicized lines taken from Parris's sermon notebook, March 27, 1691/2.

"Testimony: The Wake of History"
In his *More Wonders of the Invisible World* (1700), Robert Calef writes, "The first complain'd of, was the said Indian Woman, named Tituba. She confessed that the Devil urged her to sign a Book, which he presented to her, and also to work Mischief to the Children, etc. She was afterwards Comitted to Prison, and lay there till Sold for her Fees." The next several centuries write version after version of Tituba, transforming her from an Indian to an African woman, always insisting on her direct link with the devil.

"Testimony: The Mother"
In most histories of Salem, Dorcas Good is a footnote. The four-year-old accused her mother, Sarah Good, of witchcraft, and then because her mother was accused, the girl was considered suspect. In the seventeenth-century lexicon, choking was designated as "the suffocation of the mother," or, shortened, in common parlance, "the mother." "These swooning fits were . . . nothing else but what they call the mother" writes Sir Thomas Brown in *A Tryal of Witches of the Assizes Held at Bury*

St. Edmunds, 1682.

"Testimony: He or His Apparition"
Giles Corey is a historical personage whose identity is formed by fiction. In Henry Wadsworth Longfellow's play, *Giles Corey of Salem Farms,* Corey repeatedly asks for "more weight" as he is pressed to death with large stones, an English punishment called *peine forte and dure.*

"Archival: The Devil's Book"
Text taken from the confession of six-year-old Sarah Carrier, August 11, 1692.

"The Mather Boys"
All ministers and prolific writers, the Mathers occupy an important place in the history of the trials. Cotton Mather, the third in the Mather line, played a contradictory role in distrusting spectral evidence while believing deeply that witchcraft was spreading like a poison throughout New England.

"The People vs. Bridget Bishop, July 1999"
Historical enactments are a crucial part of present day Salem's tourist industry. Each summer, a dramatization of the trial of Bridget Bishop, titled, *Cry Innocent: The People vs. Bridget Bishop,* is a centerpiece. After one performance, I asked the actress who played Bridget about the surprising verdict. She shrugged and said nine times out of ten the tourists vote Bridget Bishop guilty and send her to be hung.

A CHRONOLOGY OF THE SALEM WITCH TRIALS

December 1691: Reverend Samuel Parris's nine-year-old daughter Elizabeth (Betty) and his eleven-year-old niece Abigail Williams are the first girls to develop symptoms. Other girls, including Ann Putnam, Mary Warren, Mercy Lewis, Mary Walcott, and Elizabeth Hubbard, then also claim to be afflicted.

February 1691/1692: Doctor Griggs cannot find any physical cause for the girls' illness and decides the Devil must be near. The girls begin to make their accusations. Tituba, Sarah Good, and Sarah Osborne are accused.

February 29: Arrest warrants are issued. The three women are held in jail. Sarah Good is pregnant. Her baby will be born in jail and die there. Her four-year-old daughter Dorcas will soon join her in jail.

March 1: The women undergo preliminary examinations by the village magistrates in the meetinghouse. Tituba confesses to practicing witchcraft. Sarah Good and Sarah Osborne say they are innocent. Throughout the trials, those who confess will not be executed—a reversal of the usual rule in witchcraft trials—but few will confess to save themselves.

March 11: A day of fasting and prayer is held to drive out the witches.

March 12–April 19: Martha Corey, Rebecca Nurse, Sarah Cloyce, Abigail Hobbs, Giles Corey, Mary Warren, and John and Elizabeth Proctor are accused of withcraft and examined.

April 22–May 10: Seventeen more people are examined.

May 10: Sarah Osborne dies in prison.

May 14: Governor Phips arrives in Salem with a new charter.

May 27: The governor sets up a Court of Oyer and Terminer ("to hear and determine").

May 31: Five more people are examined.

June 2: In the court's first session, Bridget Bishop is convicted of witchcraft and sentenced to die on June 10.

June 29–30: Five more women are tried and sentenced to die on July 19, including Sarah Good and Rebecca Nurse. Dorcas Good, who names her mother as a witch, confesses. Never formally tried, the child remains in jail for eleven months.

July 30: Captain Nathaniel Cary helps his wife Elizabeth, one of the accused, escape from jail.

August 2–6: Six more people, including John and Elizabeth Proctor, are convicted. Five will be executed August 19.

September 9–17: Fifteen more people, including Martha Corey, are sentenced to die.

September 19: Giles Corey is pressed to death.

September 22: Eight more people are hung, including Martha Corey.

October 8: Thomas Brattle writes letter criticizing the trials. Governor Phips stops the reliance on spectral evidence for conviction.

October 29: Court of Oyer and Terminer is dissolved.

1696: Twelve men who served as jurors issue a public document of apology for the trials.

1697: The Reverend Parris leaves Salem Village.

August 25, 1706: Ann Putnam, the only one of the afflicted girls to confess, publicly acknowledges her guilt with a prepared speech: *I desire to lie in the dust, and to be humbled for it, in that I was a cause, with others, of so sad a calamity to them and their families; for which cause I desire to lie in the dust, and earnestly beg forgiveness of God.*